HAL LEONARD

MANDOLIN METHOD BOOK 2

BY RICH DELGROSSO

ISBN 978-1-4803-7155-2

HAL•LEONARD®
CORPORATION
7777 W. BLUEMOUND RD. P.O. BOX 13819 MILWAUKEE, WI 53213

Copyright © 2015 by HAL LEONARD CORPORATION
International Copyright Secured   All Rights Reserved

In Australia Contact:
Hal Leonard Australia Pty. Ltd.
4 Lentara Court
Cheltenham, Victoria, 3192 Australia
Email: ausadmin@halleonard.com.au

No part of this publication may be reproduced in any form or by any means
without the prior written permission of the Publisher.

Visit Hal Leonard Online at
www.halleonard.com

CONTENTS

INTRODUCTION

Welcome to the *Hal Leonard Mandolin Method Book 2*! This set of lessons is an extension of the first book, with new skills presented in the context of a great collection of mandolin pieces representing a variety of music genres. The method continues to stress reading music in standard notation instead of tablature. This is a valuable study, as it opens your world to all of the written music available, and it isn't difficult to learn.

The genres stressed in this method are the most popular in mandolin circles: old-time, bluegrass, Celtic, classical, and blues. We begin the detailed study with an exploration of modes and scales, as they provide the foundation for melody. A study of time signatures is then relevant to the introduction of the different genres. To this point in the series, your playing has been in the first position, but now we will navigate and shift positions up the neck. This study is then applied as we take old-time music and mix it with some blues to develop the bluegrass style. The icing on the cake lies in ornamentation— those little nuanced actions on the strings that give the music its flavor. Finally, a collection of solo/duet arrangements representing the different genres is included to add to your repertoire.

Enjoy building on your skills!

SCALES AND MODES

As children, many of us learned our first musical scale using the singing syllables of **solfège**: Do–Re–Me–Fa–Sol–La–Ti–Do. These syllables represent the notes of the major scale; here it is in the key of C:

C–D–E–F–G–A–B–C

Scales are important to the study of melody. In *Hal Leonard Mandolin Method Book 1*, we studied the major scale in the keys of C, D, G, and A. These keys are easy to play because they include open string notes. Other keys, like B♭ or E, require a different fingering approach, which we will explore in this study.

Modes are related to scales. We touched on the Mixolydian mode in *Book 1*. First created by the Greeks, modes are at the root of melody development, providing a starting place for understanding music. As you will see, certain melodies are derived directly from modes.

Each mode has its own distinct pattern of whole and half step **intervals** (distances between the notes). They are all described in the following pages using the white keys of a piano or keyboard for reference.

IONIAN MODE (MAJOR SCALE)

Do–Re–Me–Fa–Sol–La–Ti–Do demonstrates the Ionian mode, which is *the same as the major scale*, and also the bedrock of the system. All other modes and scales are essentially derived from the major scale. Note in the diagram how the intervals include whole steps (W) and half steps (H). This sequence of steps is also known as the **major scale formula**. Each tone in the scale is assigned a number, or **scale degree** (listed above each note below), with the **root** note, or **tonic**, as the first degree. If you use a piano to help you, play the white keys starting with middle C:

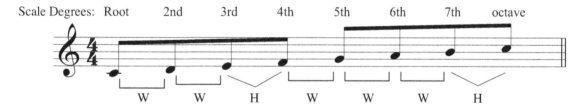

"The Wind That Shakes the Barley" is a popular Celtic reel in country dance circles, and its melody is based on the Ionian mode in the key of D. The D major scale has two sharps, F♯ and C♯, as indicated in the key signature:

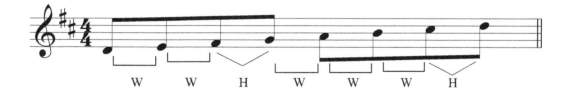

This fiddle tune, like many others, has more than one part—in this case, an A and B part. This arrangement has chords mixed into the melody to add emphasis to the rhythm. You may play it solo or with others:

THE WIND THAT SHAKES THE BARLEY

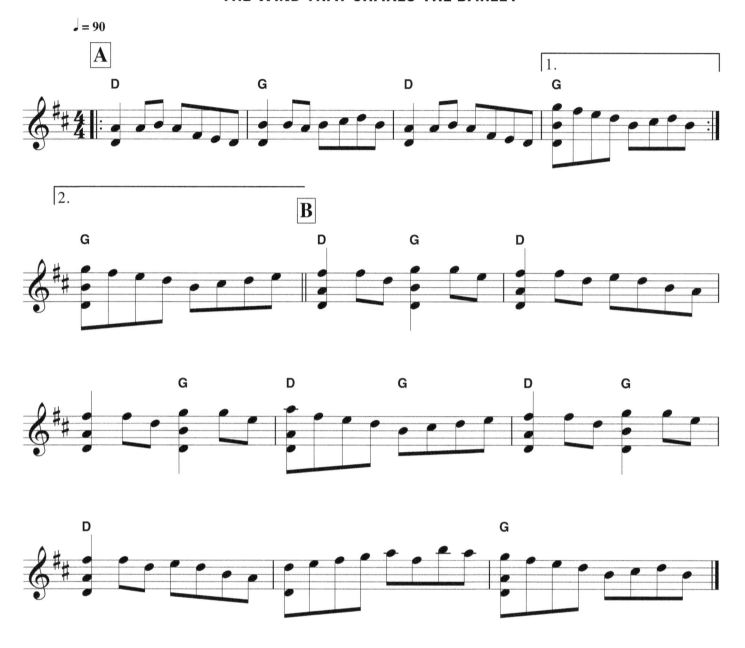

DORIAN MODE

The Dorian mode starts with the second tone of the major scale (or Ionian mode): Re. Using the C major scale, this would be the note D. You can hear the notes of this mode on the piano by starting with D and playing just the white keys in succession.

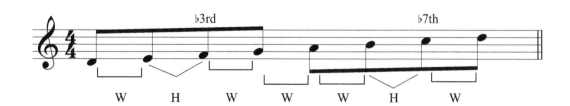

This mode is distinguished by its flatted 3rd and flatted 7th interval. It is a common mode in early American and Celtic melodies. The flatted notes create a unique melancholy—a feeling later described as "the blues." The American genre called "blues" is often a mix of Ionian and Dorian. We will explore it further in this method.

"Scarborough Fair" is an example of a melody in the Dorian mode. Here it is written as a duet for two mandolins in 3/4 time (three beats to a measure).

SCARBOROUGH FAIR

PHRYGIAN MODE

The Phrygian mode starts with the third scale degree of the major scale: Mi. Using the C major scale, this would be the note E. Again, on the piano, play the white keys starting with E.

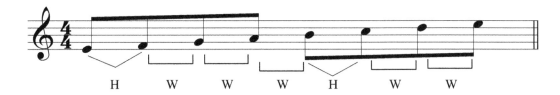

This mode is often described as having a Spanish sound and can be thought of as a substitute for the traditional minor (Aeolian) scale, but not quite as sad sounding. "Canción Para Lisa," below, was written to demonstrate the feeling of this mode, though it contains elements of other scales as well.

RITARDANDO

Notice the "rit." indication at the end of the next tune. This means **ritardando**, or to gradually slow down.

CANCIÓN PARA LISA

FREYGISH MODE (PHRYGIAN DOMINANT)

The mandolin, often regarded as a classical instrument, is now popular in a variety of styles, including blues, swing, Brazilian choro, and modern klezmer music. Klezmer, in the Jewish tradition, has a unique minor sound. Often referred to as the Phrygian dominant mode, Freygish is like the Phrygian mode but with the 3rd raised, creating a one-and-a-half step interval between the 2nd and 3rd:

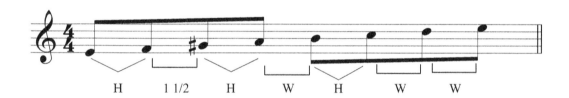

Here's the Freygish mode built from a D tonic.

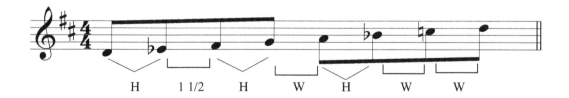

The ever-popular melody "Hava Nagila" nicely demonstrates the Freygish mode. Below is a duet for two mandolins—melody and chords.

STACCATO

Notice the dots under the noteheads in the chord part of "Hava Nagila" below. These are called **staccato** dots, and they tell you to play those notes short and detached. This is characteristic of the mandolin chop technique that you learned about in *Book 1*.

HAVA NAGILA

LYDIAN MODE

The Lydian mode belongs in the family of major-sounding modes and starts on the fourth degree of the major scale: Fa. Using the C major scale, this would be the note F. Lydian has a quirky sound due to the raised 4th (the B natural in this case):

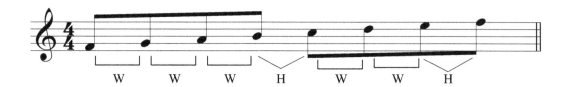

Here's the G Lydian mode.

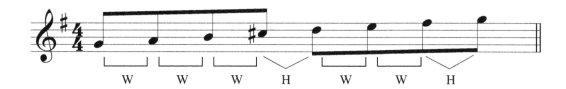

Here is a Lydian melody deep in the Scottish tradition:

THE BOB OF FETTERCAIRN

MIXOLYDIAN MODE

The Mixolydian mode belongs in the family of major-sounding modes. It starts with the fifth degree of the major scale, Sol (the note G from the C major scale), and is characterized by the flatted 7th. It is an oft-used mode in Celtic and American old-time music.

Here's the A Mixolydian mode.

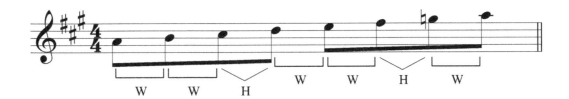

"Kitchen Girl" is a popular American fiddle tune that demonstrates the Mixolydian mode. This arrangement is a duet for melody and chords. The indicated metronome marking (54 bpm) is a good speed, or **tempo**, for practice, but raise it up by 10 bpm when you are ready to perform it.

KITCHEN GIRL

AEOLIAN MODE (MINOR SCALE)

The Aeolian mode is the most recognized in the family of minor-sounding modes. It is the *same as the natural minor scale* and is built from the sixth degree of the major scale: La.

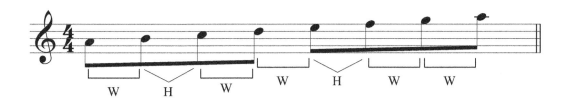

"Greensleeves" is one of the most popular Aeolian mode melodies ever. Here is a duet for two mandolins in A Aeolian. Notice that the natural 6th and 7th (F# and G#, respectively) appear along with the mode's flatted 6th and 7th tones. This could be interpreted as the **melodic minor scale**, a variation of the natural minor scale.

GREENSLEEVES

LOCRIAN MODE

The Locrian mode is built from the seventh degree of the major scale: Ti (B in C major).

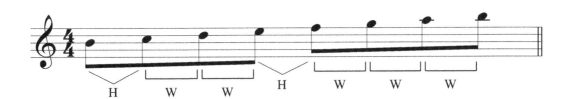

The Locrian mode isn't typically used in traditional music, but you should be aware of its existence. This mode is sometimes used in creating transitions and short passages in classical and jazz music. It's a very "theoretical" mode and creates the minor seventh flat five chord.

TIME SIGNATURES

In the mandolin world today, you will encounter music of many different cultures and genres. Some, like Neapolitan dance music and American blues and bluegrass, have longstanding popularity. Celtic, Brazilian choro music, jazz, swing, and even Jewish klezmer music played on the mandolin are fairly recent rages. Even though the instrument is not associated with these styles in their traditions, the mandolin is welcomed widely. These genres vary in arrangement style, melody, phrasing, and use of modes and scales. They also stress different rhythms.

Our study of rhythm begins with the time signature that is indicated at the beginning of the music staff—a concept that was touched on in *Book 1*.

4/4 AND 2/4

4/4 time, or common time, indicates four beats per measure, with a quarter note representing one beat. Try this "boogie bass" line for a simple 4/4 rhythm. You can play this with simple downstrokes.

BOOGIE BASS

"Old French" is a popular reel in 4/4 time with eighth notes. You play them with alternating downstrokes and upstrokes, even as you change strings. This pattern creates a nice flow that helps you to increase the speed of your playing.

Note: This arrangement includes an ABA song form and a mix of modes. The melody in the A part comes from the D Ionian mode, while the B part changes to A Mixolydian.

OLD FRENCH

2/4 time has a different feel than 4/4, as it has an inherent bounce to it. A polka is a perfect example. Many cultures have polkas in their dance tradition. "Dennis Murphy's Polka" is a Celtic polka.

DENNIS MURPHY'S POLKA

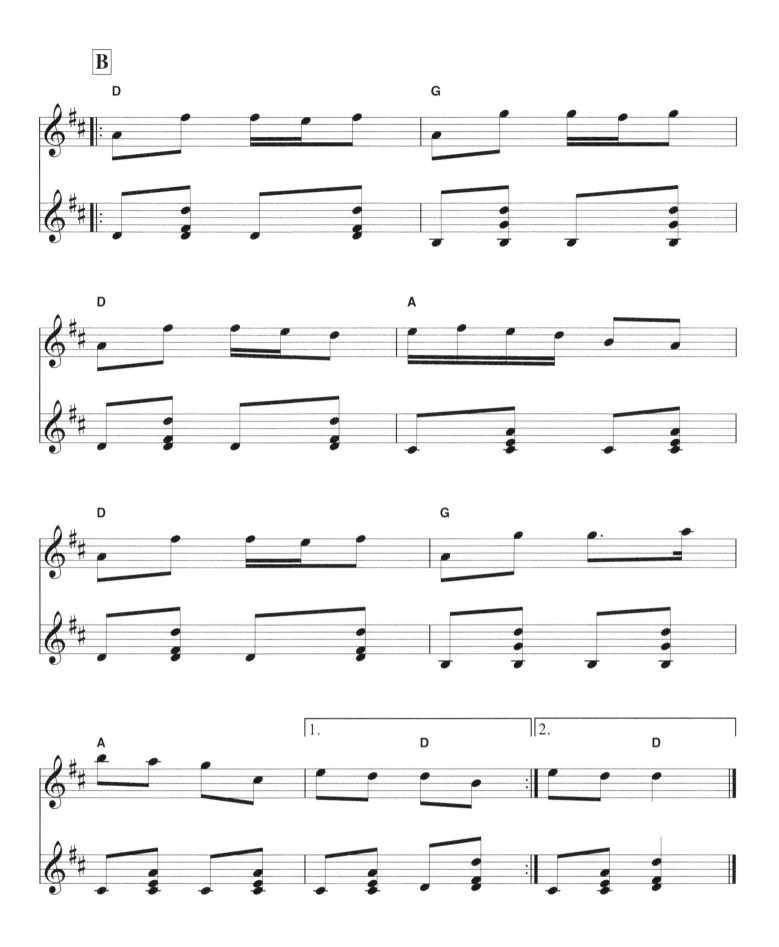

In the Celtic or Irish step dance tradition there are four rhythms: the **reel**, the **jig**, the **slip jig**, and the **hornpipe**. The hornpipe rhythm is cast in 2/4 time with strategic triplets that give it a skipping rhythm. Play it with the down/up alternate picking style.

"The Boys of Bluehill" is a popular hornpipe in New England dance circles. For the chord part, play the D chord in third position (see the "Transposing" section on page 32 for more on fretboard positions), with your ring finger on the fourth string, seventh fret. The A chord is best played with a barre at the second fret.

SHUFFLE OR SWING FEEL

The next song is played with a slight "lilt" or "bounce" to the eighth-note rhythms, in which the first of each pair of notes is elongated and the second is shortened, resulting in an uneven, triplet-based rhythmic flow. This is known as **shuffle feel** (or **swing feel**) and is common in many forms of music, from Irish to blues to jazz and rock.

THE BOYS OF BLUEHILL

In "Freylekhs," melody notes on the upbeats provide syncopation. Note the melody in the first measure—you rest on the downbeat (when your foot taps down) and pick the note on the upbeat (when your foot rises).

FREYLEKHS

3/4

3/4 time is most often associated with waltz rhythm—three beats to a measure. This arrangement of the Neapolitan waltz, "Veni Sul Mare," features parts for two mandolins.

VENI SUL MARE

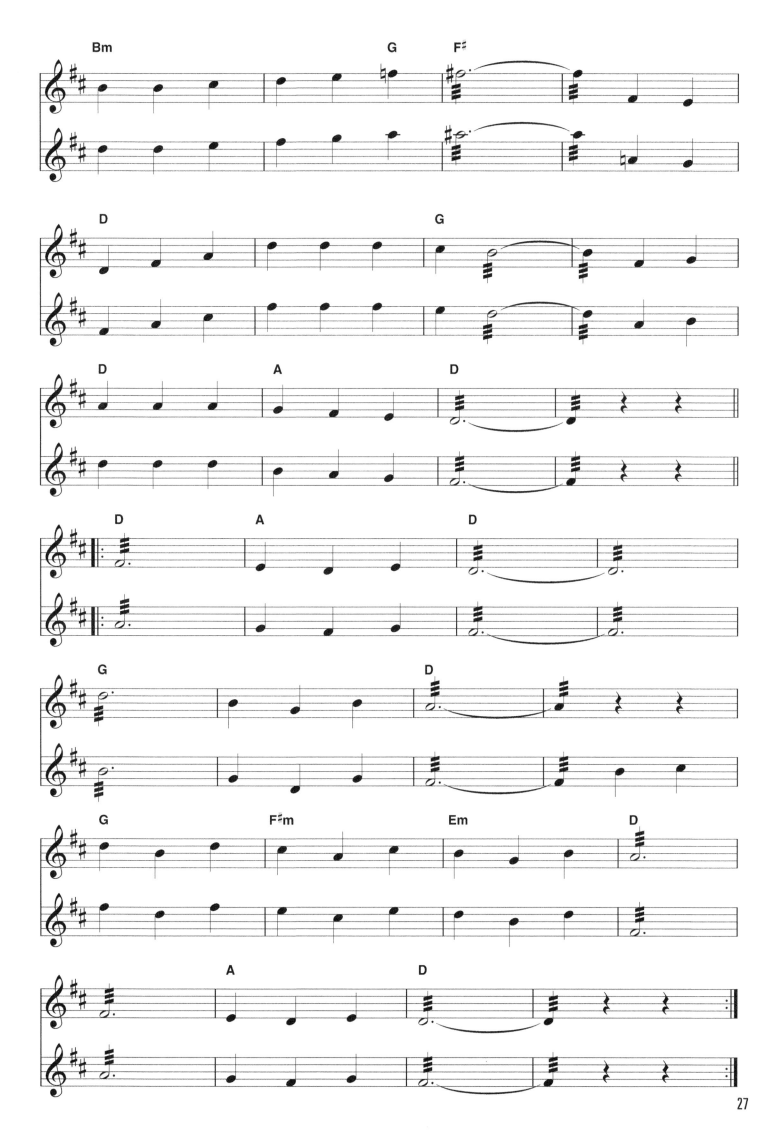

6/8

In 6/8 time, your foot taps as if it were 2/4 time, but each beat is divided into a triplet of eighth notes. This is the rhythm of many dances, as varied as the Celtic jig and the Italian tarantella.

"Banish Misfortune" is a personal favorite, and this arrangement comes from playing with Celtic musicians in Detroit, where I grew up. It is a two-part arrangement with a melody based on the Mixolydian mode.

BANISH MISFORTUNE

"Cicerenella" is a Neapolitan tarantella, a fast-paced dance popularized in southern Italy. A second mandolin part is added to this arrangement to capture the rhythm.

CICERENELLA

9/8

The best example of **9/8 time** is the music of the Irish slip jig, the quickest-paced step dance—graceful and very controlled.

KID ON THE MOUNTAIN

TRANSPOSING

TRANSPOSING VERTICALLY

The tuning of the mandolin and its sister, the violin, to G–D–A–E is not accidental. Tuning the strings in 5ths enables one to **transpose** easily (move from one key to another) by shifting to different strings while your hand remains in the same position on the neck.

Position describes the placement of your fretting hand and fingers on the mandolin neck. For example, in "first position" your hand is positioned so that your index finger plays the notes on the first or second frets. Likewise, you use your middle finger to fret notes at the second or third fret, your ring finger to fret notes at the fourth or fifth fret, and your pinky to fret notes at the sixth fret. Open notes are also included in this position.

While playing in first position, you can easily transpose a melody to its 5th in the scale. "Midnight on the Water" is a popular Texan waltz, written here in the key of G.

MIDNIGHT ON THE WATER (IN G)

To transpose this melody to the key of D (the 5th of G), simply shift your fingers to the next set of strings.

MIDNIGHT ON THE WATER (IN D)

You are reading the notes, but your fingers are playing the same pattern on adjacent strings.

TRANSPOSING HORIZONTALLY: CHANGING POSITION

To play "Midnight on the Water" in the key of E calls for a different type of transposition involving a horizontal change in position. In the key of D, this melody starts on an open note (D), and the A and E are also played on open strings. But in the key of E, the melody starts with E on the third string, second fret.

The E major scale begins with this note and is played in **closed position**—i.e., without open strings. You need to use all four fingers to play the E major scale. Watch as you play. The first four notes of the scale form a pattern that is repeated on the next string up:

Now play "Midnight on the Water" in the key of E. Both tablature and fingerings are provided here so you can see the position clearly. It will take time to adjust to the fingering. As you practice the previous scale exercise, you will find the melody easier to play.

MIDNIGHT ON THE WATER (IN E)

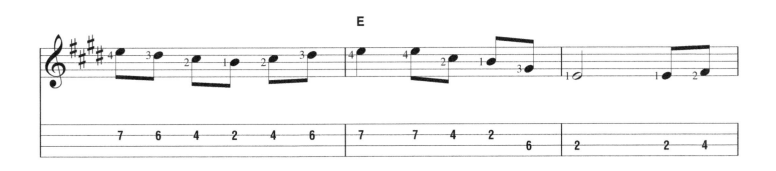

Let's explore this transposition technique using an arrangement of "Angeline the Baker" from *Book 1*. The arrangement is in G Ionian in the first position.

ANGELINE THE BAKER (IN G)

0 = OPEN	
1 = INDEX	
2 = MIDDLE	
3 = RING	
4 = PINKY	

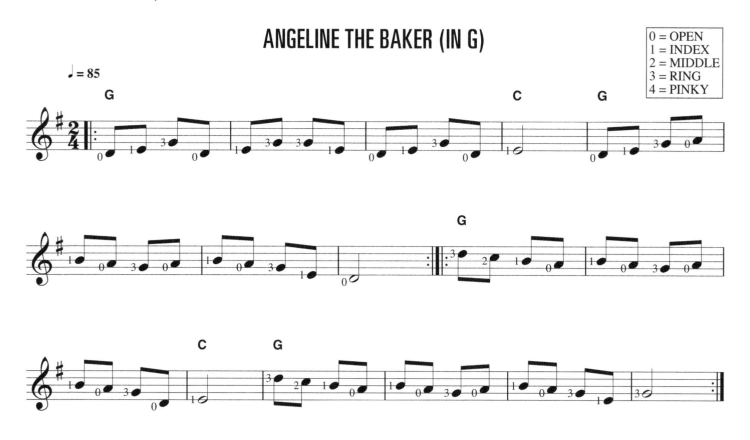

Now shift a bit in the first position and play it in E Ionian. The E and A in the melody could be played as open notes, but for the purposes of this lesson, use your pinky to play these as fretted notes instead. Practice the stretch to get the notes. It helps if you pull your elbow closer to your body, placing your hand at an angle to facilitate the stretch. It will take some time to adjust, but playing scales this way will train your fretting hand and enable you to play in any key.

ANGELINE THE BAKER (IN E)

"Golden Slippers" is another tune from *Book 1* in the key of D. It is also easily played in A in the first position.

GOLDEN SLIPPERS (IN A)

"Slippers" in C

To transpose "Slippers" to the key of C, change to second position. Move your hand up the neck (towards the body) until your index finger plays notes at the third fret (the area of the neck that was covered by your middle, or "second" finger—hence, the "second" position).

The melody in the A part is played on the second string. The B part includes notes played on the third string. The pinky stretch here will feel like even more of a challenge, but it is worth the effort. Start with the scale below, where middle C is played with the middle finger.

Note that in the key of C arrangement of "Golden Slippers," you have two possible choices for playing B. In measure 4, playing the quick sixteenth note at the ninth fret slows the flow, so I decided to play it at the second fret. But in the fifth measure of the B part (as well as the fourth measure from the end), I find it easier to play by adjusting my hand position slightly forward and playing it with my pinky. This is called **shifting**.

GOLDEN SLIPPERS (IN C)

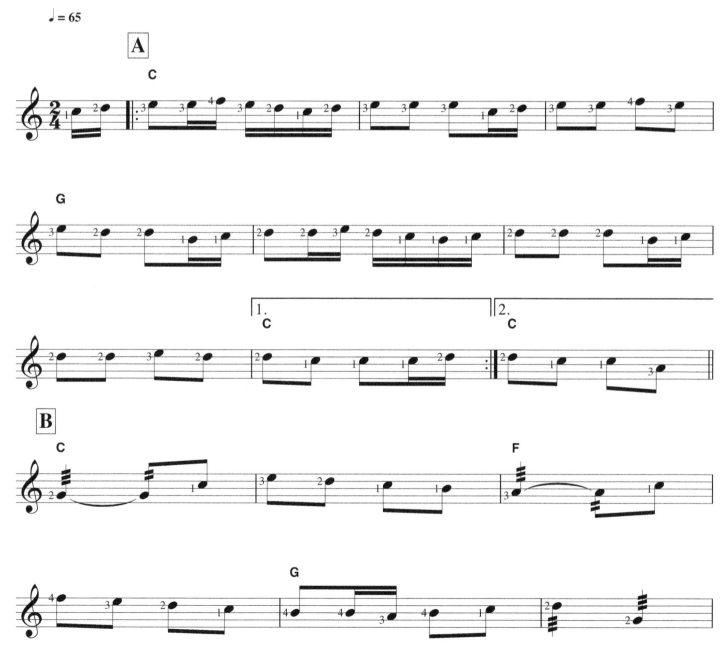

SHIFTING: CHANGING POSITION TO FACILITATE PLAYING

In addition to transposing to different keys, changing hand position can facilitate easier and more efficient playing, as you saw in the previous song example. Some melodies appear to be awkward at first until you figure out logical ways to change hand position—i.e., when and where to shift. Then the melody just flows effortlessly. The following scales and arrangements have the fingering notated to demonstrate how shifting works.

Practice the key of G major scale below to develop a sense of position. Start with the open G. When you reach the first octave on the third string, quickly change the position of your hand and play this note with your index finger. Your hand adjusts upward into third position. This is indicated by your index finger when playing a note that is usually fretted by your third, or ring, finger in first position:

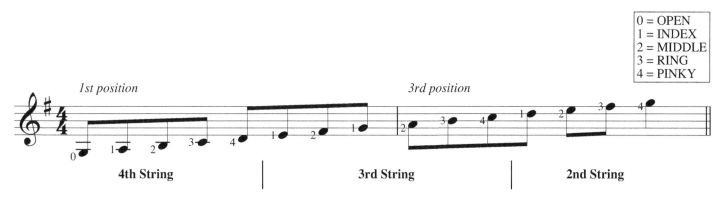

Do the same in the key of D:

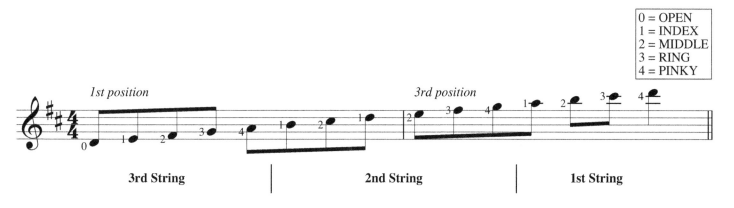

The following arrangements all feature melody segments that are played with shifting.

The "Jenny Lind Polka" is played in first position, but the opening phrase has more life if you play it on the middle two strings, shifting from fourth to second to first positions. Play this phrase using downstrokes. When you play it again in measure 5, use down-up-down strokes to add the extra sixteenth note.

JENNY LIND POLKA

Shifting position in the B part of "Jenny Pippin" is a must. The D scale in the third position, starting on the second string, sets you up for effortless execution of what appears to be a complex melody. At the end of the second ending, jump up to third position and use your index finger to barre both the second and first strings. The most difficult maneuver begins in the fourth measure of the B part, as the melody shifts to the third string and then back to the second. Fret the F# with your ring finger and the G with your pinky. This will take some practice.

JENNY PIPPIN

Execution of "La Bastringue" has elements of the previous two arrangements. This time, as you play the opening phrase of the B part, hold the barre on the first two strings for each phrase, changing position from the fifth fret (third position) to the third fret (second position). The open E frees up your hand to shift down to first position. The melody cascades down. Follow the fingering and the notes will flow.

LA BASTRINGUE

The "Ash Grove" is a solo piece played with doublestops to fill out the melody. Doublestops were covered in *Book 1* and are partial chords consisting of only two notes. Use a barre on the first and second strings to play the F#/B doublestops for the Bm chord. Matching a harmony note to a melody note in the B part requires a change in hand position. Use the quarter rest in the second ending to release your hand and jump up to third position, fretting with your ring finger on the second string, ninth fret. The doublestops are stretches—over five frets! Fret them with your index and ring fingers.

THE ASH GROVE

"Planxty Irwin," played in 6/8, has a different feel than the traditional jig. Turlough O'Carolan was a famous Irish harpist and composer in the early 1700s who composed melodies (that he called **planxtys**) in tribute to his benefactors—in this case, Colonel John Irwin of Sligo. Fingering shifts are notated in the arrangement.

PLANXTY IRWIN

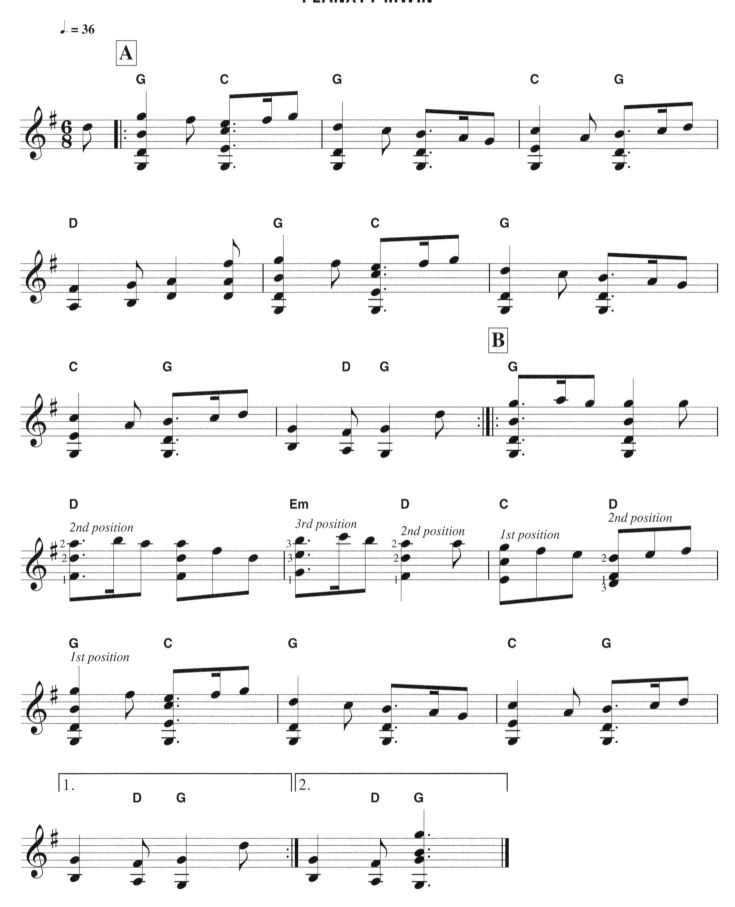

Now you have the basic idea. Explore other melodies for shifting possibilities, and your playing will be transformed!

BLUES

The story of the mandolin in America began in the mid 1800s, as Italian immigrants brought mandolins to the New World and the luthiers among them were hired by U.S. companies to produce Neapolitan-style mandolins. By the 1920s, the mandolin reached fad status, especially with the player-friendly flat-back design created by Orville Gibson. The mandolin gained in popularity among the string and jug band performers, and as W.C. Handy recalled in his writing, one of his first encounters with the "blues" was played by a mandolin player in a trio in 1903. The mandolin has been in the blues since the blues began!

In defining any genre of music, you consider four basic elements: melody, harmony, rhythm, and arrangement.

A blues melody is born from the **major pentatonic scale** of West African music—the music the slaves brought to the New World. As the name implies, it is a scale based on five notes, as demonstrated in this C major pentatonic scale:

Major Pentatonic Scale

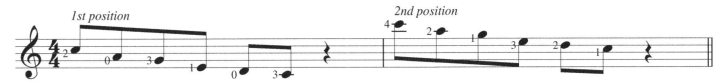

The pentatonic scale has a unique flavor and importance, as it is the bedrock for the music of Asia, Africa, and Native America.

There is also a **minor pentatonic scale** that is similar to the Dorian mode, with flatted 3rd and flatted 7th scale tones.

Minor Pentatonic Scale

It is the minor pentatonic scale that is at the root of African-American music. Blended with the European major scale, the **composite blues scale** emerges. It is the essence of blues, rhythm and blues, jazz, rock 'n' roll, zydeco, soul, bluegrass, rap, hip hop, and modern country.

Composite Blues Scale

In the C composite blues scale, the flatted 3rd (E♭), 5th (G♭), and 7th (B♭) intervals in the scale are called the "blue notes." Alternating these flatted tones with their natural counterparts creates what is called the "blues inflection." The blues artist hears, and desires, a note between the flatted note and the natural. Singers and guitarists **bend** a note to find it. Mandolins and fiddles **slide** into the note, indicated by slanted lines angled upward or downward into the notehead, or like piano players, they will play the flatted and natural note together—a technique called a **smear** (see "Blues in C," measure 5). These actions create a dissonance in the music, and that's what makes the blues.

Adding a flatted 7th in the melody requires the same in its harmony, so depending on the melody, you frequently play what are called **7th chords**, or **dominant chords**. Watch for these new types of chords in the next example.

The beat of the blues is the **backbeat** (also known as the "upbeat"). There are two ways to feel the backbeat. In 4/4 time, a single beat may be divided into two eighth notes. The backbeat is the second of the two. In a blues melody, phrases often start on the backbeat (as you can see in measures 3, 7, and 10 of "Blues in C"). Musicians often describe the backbeat another way, by accenting beats 2 and 4, as demonstrated in the chord part for "Blues in C." The bottom mandolin part sets the rhythm with strong chords on the backbeat.

The most common song form in the blues consists of twelve measures (or bars) that repeat until the end. "Blues in C" is a **12-bar blues**.

BLUES IN C

BLUEGRASS

The popularity of Bill Monroe and the Bluegrass Boys in the '30s spotlighted the band's unique vocal style and Monroe's primary instrument, the mandolin. The band, from the bluegrass state of Kentucky, popularized a new style of music later named "bluegrass." Monroe's music was born out the influence of his uncle Pendleton "Uncle Penn" Vandiver, who introduced him to Scottish and Irish fiddle tunes, and guitarist/fiddler Arnold Schultz, who brought him the blues. Bluegrass is a blend of the rhythm of dance tunes with expressive, blues-infused melodies. This genre is unique and a favorite of string band musicians.

The rhythm of bluegrass is often fast-paced, rolling like the hills, with support that rhythm guitar players call the "boom chang." In an attempt to provide a drum-like rhythm, the guitar and/or bass thumps on the downbeat like a kick drum, and the mandolin "chops" on the backbeat like a snare.

The classic mandolin chop (discussed in *Book 1*) is played with four-finger chords. Below are three examples shown in notation and tablature:

Four-Finger Chords

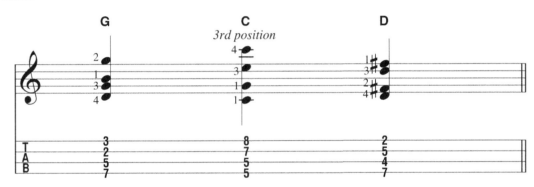

The finger stretch of these chords on the fingerboard can be daunting. Three-finger variations are often substituted. Below are three examples:

Three-Finger Variations

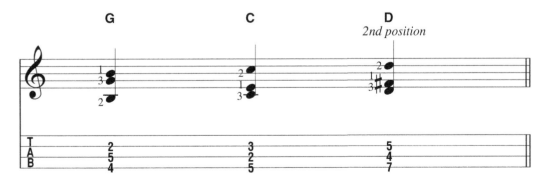

To create the chop sound, strike a chord with a single downstroke on the backbeat, then lift your fingers slightly to choke off the sound. The chop is percussive.

Bluegrass Chop

The melody of a bluegrass instrumental can flow like a current and is often very fast, so you need to develop a picking hand action that some call "constant motion." Your wrist is loose—don't pick from your forearm. It's all in the wrist. Practice with this next exercise. The first line starts with a downstroke and then a down-up on the backbeat. The second line is a double down-up motion. It's like playing a slow-motion tremolo.

Bluegrass Exercise

Bluegrass developed out of the early string band tradition, so let's take an old-time tune like "Little Liza Jane" and convert it to bluegrass. First practice the melody until it plays smooth and easy.

SIXTEENTH-NOTE TRIPLETS

The next song includes a new rhythm: the **sixteenth-note triplet**:

This type of triplet divides an eighth note into three equal parts, in the same way an eighth-note triplet divides a quarter note into three equal parts.

You'll often see a sixteenth-note triplet beamed together with other rhythms, like this:

LITTLE LIZA JANE

Now give it the bluegrass touch. A good "kick off" gets the rhythm rolling with extra notes added in to keep the music flowing. This will take time and practice, but soon it will be a roller coaster and just as much fun.

The second mandolin part covers the rhythm chop as described earlier. The Bm requires a barre on the third and fourth strings in second position. The A chord is formed by barring the third and fourth strings in first position.

LITTLE LIZA JANE—Bluegrass Style

Now give the arrangement additional punch by adding blue notes to the melody.

LITTLE LIZA JANE—Bluegrass Style Variation

ORNAMENTATION

In music, **ornaments**, or **embellishments**, are notes and flourishes that are not part of the melody but are added to decorate, or "ornament," the melody line. They are basic to classical music, varying in use by composers. In the folk music realm, the use of ornamentation may vary by genre—i.e., **slides**, **hammer-ons**, and **pull-offs** are common in the blues, while **mordents**, **turns**, **trebles**, and **trills** are common in the early American and Celtic traditions. In standard music notation, a common ornament is indicated by its specific symbol, or a composer may add ornamentation by including the notes themselves. The common ornaments are described and performed below:

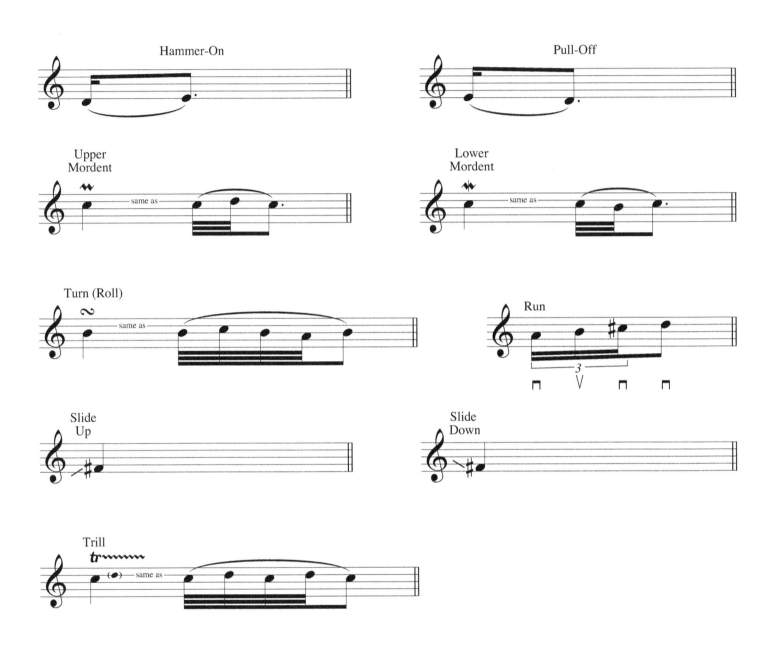

Hammer-ons are played with two or more notes that sound from only one pick stroke. For the hammer-on in the example above, pick the open D string and then fret, or "hammer," the E with your index finger. The notes change without having to pick the E. Hammer-ons can also be performed with all fretted notes along the same string.

Pull-offs are similar to hammer-ons, but they are opposite in execution. Fret the E and hold it in place. After you pick the E, lift your finger off to sound the open D string. As you lift from the E, use your finger to pull at the string. This will make the effect stronger. In a sense, you are softly picking the string with your fretting finger. Like hammer-ons, pull-offs can also be performed with all fretted notes along the same string.

The hammer-on/ pull-off technique is the foundation of most of the ornamentation described above.

In "Sandy River Belle," I have created an arrangement that includes both hammer-ons and pull-offs, indicated by slurs in the notation.

SANDY RIVER BELLE

With a turn or "roll," the melody pauses on a given note and does a somersault, interrupting the flow of notes for more interest and character. The turn has five notes on the beat so it must flow effortlessly. Broken down, a turn is a hammer-on followed by two pull-offs and another hammer-on.

The mordents, upper and lower, are similar but abbreviated versions of the turn, involving just a hammer-on and pull-off with a note above (upper), or a pull-off and hammer-on with a note below (lower). Consult the previous ornamentation diagram for descriptions and examples of each one.

"Lark in the Morning" is a popular Irish jig that was first introduced in *Hal Leonard Mandolin Method Book 1*. This reprise is designed to add ornaments that give the arrangement more authenticity as a Celtic tune. The first eight bars are without ornamentation to contrast the before and after.

You can play the B part in the first position, but you may find that it rolls off the fingers better if you play in the third position. Try both!

LARK IN THE MORNING

The **run** is a series of notes that are essentially pickup notes leading into another phrase. The arrangement to "Little Liza Jane" featured runs. In "Fisher's Hornpipe," the runs in the A part add lift to the melody.

Notice the "shuffle feel" indication at the top of the song, a rhythmic concept first discussed on page 22. In this case, the shuffle feel is added to the sixteenth notes instead of eighth notes.

FISHER'S HORNPIPE

The **slide** and **trill** give this next "Blues Duet" additional feeling. Slides were discussed earlier and also in *Book 1*. In this song, the slides start one fret below the note to be played. The trill is a substitute for tremolo; this is a rapid, repeated hammer-on/ pull-off move between the note indicated and a note above it. Here, you trill the open A with the C natural.

In measure 5 of the second mandolin part, the sustained, tremolo-picked tones slowly walk the G7 harmony down to the tonic chord, D7. The G# under the G7 in measure 10 creates a dissonant harmony that is all blues!

BLUES DUET

MORE SOLOS AND DUETS

The following is a collection of solos and duets that reflect back on the lessons in this book.

"Musette" is a beautiful piece by Bach for piano. Here the parts are split up for two mandolins. It is a sweet tune with a lot of lift that doesn't call for ornamentation.

FERMATA

The symbol near the end of the next piece in the second mandolin part is called a **fermata** (or **hold**). It calls for the music to pause briefly until you decide to move forward.

MUSETTE

"Star of the County Down" is a classic Irish ballad that is performed at a fast tempo when sung, but makes a beautiful duet ballad when played at a modest tempo. This arrangement includes very little ornamentation in the melody, though some tremolo is added in a few spots. Positions are noted for the chord part in the opening bars to get you started.

STAR OF THE COUNTY DOWN

"Jug Band Blues" revisits the basic blues elements, including slides between the blue notes (flatted notes) and their natural counterparts. And in '20s style, this arrangement of the 12-bar blues is unique because of its transition in measure 6 to a **diminished 7th chord** (C#°7). This is a minor-sounding chord type featuring a flatted 5th and **double-flatted** 7th (in this case, the B♭).

JUG BAND BLUES

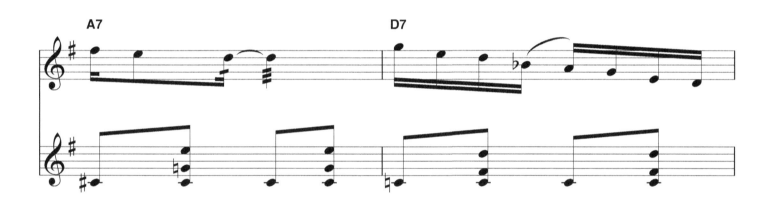

The old-time classic "Old Joe Clark," first introduced in *Book 1*, is presented here in a bluegrass style. The lines, derived from the Mixolydian mode, flow as continuous sixteenth notes with occasional changes in rhythm, like changing gears. Blue notes—the flatted 3rd (F♮), flatted 5th (A♭ or G♯), and flatted 7th (C♮)—also contribute to the bluegrass spice. Practice it slowly at first. Once you can play it cleanly, then gradually build up speed.

OLD JOE CLARK—Bluegrass Style

The "Dill Pickle Rag" was written by Charles Johnson in 1906. It is a classic rag that has been interpreted in many different ways over the years. Like most rags, it is made of three parts. Note how the shifting allows for smooth fingering on the melody. The shifting also helps the second mandolin work through the cycle of chords at the end of the piece.

DILL PICKLE RAG

And finally, we'll end with the most challenging piece, the traditional Spanish flamenco "Malagueña." It is a perfect study of the Phrygian mode. It starts in Ionian but quickly shifts to pure Phrygian. It has various changes in tempo and gradually picks up speed. The fermatas temporarily stop the flow to heighten the anticipation of the next part. Have fun!

MALAGUEÑA

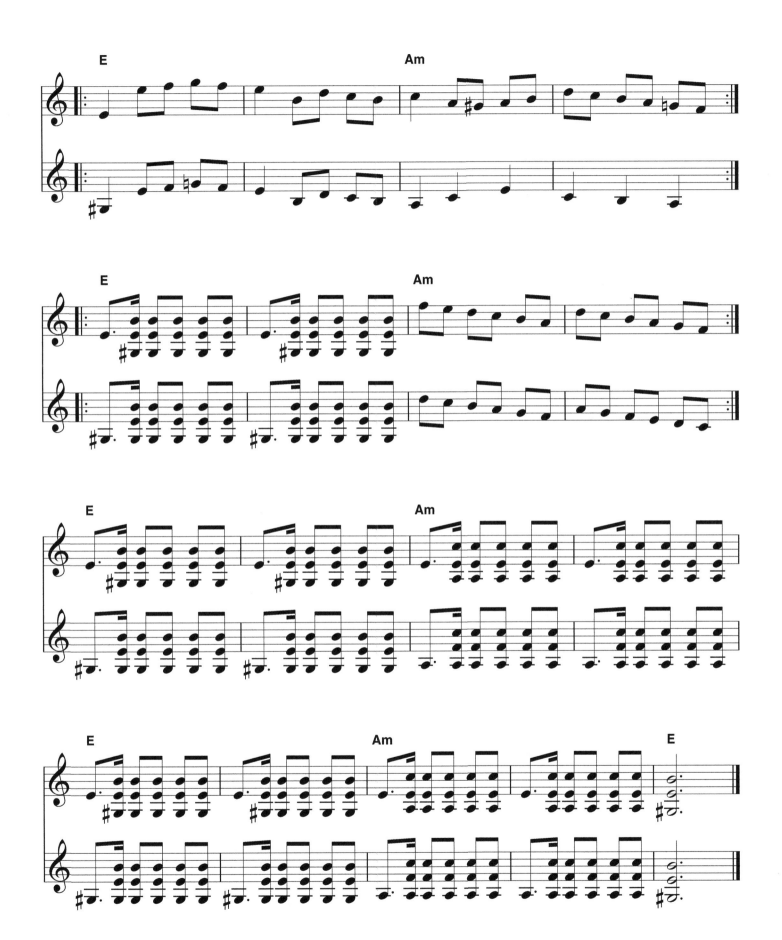

Great Mandolin Songbooks
from Hal Leonard

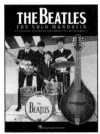

THE BEATLES FOR SOLO MANDOLIN

20 favorite Beatles tunes in chord melody arrangements for mandolin including: All You Need Is Love • Blackbird • Can't Buy Me Love • Eight Days a Week • Here Comes the Sun • Hey Jude • In My Life • Let It Be • Michelle • Strawberry Fields Forever • Twist and Shout • We Can Work It Out • Yesterday • and more.
00128672..........................$16.99

CHRISTMAS CAROLS FOR MANDOLIN

23 Christmas songs arranged especially for mandolin, including: Away in a Manger • The First Noel • God Rest Ye Merry, Gentlemen • Hark! the Herald Angels Sing • It Came upon the Midnight Clear • Jingle Bells • O Christmas Tree • O Holy Night • Silent Night • Up on the Housetop • We Wish You a Merry Christmas • What Child Is This? • and more.
00699800..........................$10.99

CLASSICAL SOLOS FOR MANDOLIN

This publication contains 20 classical mandolin pieces compiled, edited, and performed by world-renowned virtuoso Carlos Aonzo. The music is arranged in order of difficulty beginning with exercises by Giuseppe Branzoli and finishing with complete concert pieces using the most advanced mandolin techniques. Pieces include: Andante – Pizzicato on the Left Hand (Carlo Munier) • Exercise in A Major (Giuseppe Branzoli) • La Fustemberg (Antonio Riggeiri) • Partita V in G minor Overture (Filippo Sauli) • Theme with Variations in A Major (Bartolomeo Bortolazzi) • and more.
00124955 Book/Online Audio..........................$19.99

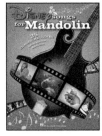

DISNEY SONGS FOR MANDOLIN

25 classic melodies from Disney's finest productions over the years presented in arrangements for mandolin. Includes: The Bare Necessities • Be Our Guest • Circle of Life • Colors of the Wind • Go the Distance • Heigh-Ho • It's a Small World • Mickey Mouse March • A Spoonful of Sugar • Under the Sea • When You Wish upon a Star • Zip-A-Dee-Doo-Dah • and more.
00701904..........................$12.99

FIDDLE TUNES FOR FLATPICKERS: MANDOLIN

Now you can learn to play famous fiddle tunes specially arranged for mandolin. Get started flatpickin' now with songs like: Blackberry Blossom • Kentucky Mandolin • Old Joe Clark • Salt Creek • Turkey in the Straw • and more. The accompanying audio features specially mixed tracks that let you hear the mandolin alone, the mandolin with the backing track, or just the backing track so you can play along!
14011276 Book/Online Audio..........................$17.99

FIRST 50 SONGS YOU SHOULD PLAY ON MANDOLIN

A fantastic collection of 50 accessible, must-know favorites for the beginner who's learned enough to start playing popular songs: Amazing Grace • Crazy • Cripple Creek • Folsom Prison Blues • Friend of the Devil • Hallelujah • Ho Hey • I Am a Man of Constant Sorrow • I Walk the Line • I'll Fly Away • Losing My Religion • Maggie May • Mr. Bojangles • Rocky Top • Take Me Home, Country Roads • Tennessee Waltz • Wagon Wheel • Wildwood Flower • Yesterday • and more.
00155489 Tab, Chords & Lyrics..........................$15.99

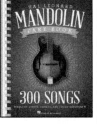

FOLK SONGS FOR MANDOLIN

SING, STRUM & PICK ALONG
More than 40 traditional favorites arranged specifically for mandolin: Arkansas Traveler • Buffalo Gals • (I Wish I Was In) Dixie • Home on the Range • I've Been Working on the Railroad • Man of Constant Sorrow • Michael Row the Boat Ashore • My Old Kentucky Home • Oh! Susanna • She'll Be Comin' 'Round the Mountain • Turkey in the Straw • The Wabash Cannon Ball • When the Saints Go Marching In • Yankee Doodle • and more!
00701918..........................$16.99

THE HAL LEONARD MANDOLIN FAKE BOOK

This collection packs 300 songs into one handy songbook: As Time Goes By • Bad, Bad Leroy Brown • Can't Take My Eyes off of You • Daydream Believer • Edelweiss • Fields of Gold • Going to California • Hey, Soul Sister • Ho Hey • I'm Yours • Island in the Sun • King of the Road • Losing My Religion • Maggie May • Over the Rainbow • Peaceful Easy Feeling • Redemption Song • Shenandoah • Toes • Unchained Melody • Wildwood Flower • You Are My Sunshine • and many more.
00141053 Melody, Lyrics & Chords..............$39.99

MASTERS OF THE MANDOLIN

This collection of 130 mandolin solos is an invaluable resource for fans of bluegrass music. Each song excerpt has been meticulously transcribed note-for-note in tab from its original recording so you can study and learn these masterful solos by some of the instrument's finest pickers. From the legendary Bill Monroe to more contemporary heroes like Sam Bush and Chris Thile, and even including some non-bluegrass greats like Dave Apollon and Jethro Burns, this book contains a wide variety of music and playing styles to enjoy.
00195621..........................$24.99

THE MIGHTY MANDOLIN CHORD SONGBOOK

Lyrics, chord symbols, and mandolin chord diagrams for 100 pop and rock hits: Blowin' in the Wind • Crazy Little Thing Called Love • Dance with Me • Edelweiss • Georgia on My Mind • Hey Jude • I Feel the Earth Move • Jolene • Lean on Me • Me and Bobby McGee • Mean • No Woman No Cry • Patience • Ring of Fire • Sweet Caroline • This Land Is Your Land • Unchained Melody • Wonderwall • and many more.
00123221..........................$17.99

O BROTHER, WHERE ART THOU?

This collection contains both note-for-note transcribed mandolin solos, as well as mandolin arrangements of the melody lines for 11 songs: Angel Band • The Big Rock Candy Mountain • Down to the River to Pray • I Am a Man of Constant Sorrow • I Am Weary (Let Me Rest) • I'll Fly Away • In the Highways (I'll Be Somewhere Working for My Lord) • In the Jailhouse Now • Indian War Whoop • Keep on the Sunny Side • You Are My Sunshine.
00695762 Tab, Chords & Lyrics..........................$15.99

THE ULTIMATE MANDOLIN SONGBOOK

arr. Janet Davis
The Ultimate Mandolin Songbook contains multiple versions varying in difficulty of 26 of the most popular songs from bluegrass, jazz, ragtime, rock, pop, gospel, swing and other genres, in both standard notation and mandolin tab. Songs: Alabama Jubilee • Autumn Leaves • The Entertainer • Great Balls of Fire • How Great Thou Art • Limehouse Blues • Orange Blossom Special • Rawhide • Stardust • Tennessee Waltz • Yesterday • You Are My Sunshine • and more!
00699913 Book/Online Audio..........................$34.99

HAL•LEONARD®

For more info, songlists, or to purchase these and more books from your favorite music retailer, go to
halleonard.com

Prices, contents and availability are subject to change without notice.
Disney characters and artwork TM & © 2021 Disney

0321
252